A Physics for People

Snooks,
Snorks,
and
Sneeples!

AN
EDUCATIONAL
PARODY

by **J.G.Kemp**
(as Dr. SNOYT)

From QUARKS to SNORKS
to clusters of FLUFF
to the *blackest* BLACK-HOLES
and other fun stuff . . .

There are things that we know,
great things we've uncovered,
MARVELOUS, WONDERFUL
things we've discovered!

Let me share them with you,
I know you will find
that it's MARVELOUS,
WONDERFUL
food for the mind!

"DR. SNOYT, this is *great!*
I'm ready to know!
Start up this
ASTROPHYSICS show!"

MARVELOUS! WONDERFUL!
Hop in my car,
and I'll teach you, my friend,
how to build a STAR!

Let's begin with the fact
that we're *stuck* to this Earth,
weighed down to the ground
by a force that is worth
even *more* when something
is made of more MASS,
like the ten-mile tail
of a giant ZONG-ZASS.

The more *stuff* there is
the stronger the force,
this is why mountains
weigh more than a horse,
or why a cloud of stuff
up in space
gets all pulled-together
in the first place.

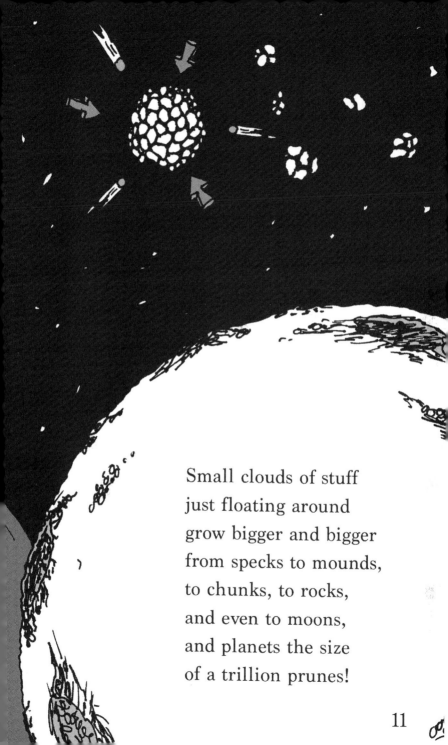

Small clouds of stuff
just floating around
grow bigger and bigger
from specks to mounds,
to chunks, to rocks,
and even to moons,
and planets the size
of a trillion prunes!

11

Now keep adding stuff!
More and MORE!
More and more mass,
more than before!
And stronger and stronger
the force it becomes,
with every speck
with every crumb!

A million EARTHS
could fit in our SUN,
or maybe even
a million and *one!*

13

Bigger and
BIGGER and
BIGGER, I say!
And suddenly night
ignites into day!
So much mass
has built us a STAR
that is bigger and brighter
than even these GNAR!

14

AR

As we added
more mass,
row by row,
that force
(call it GRAVITY),
strong did it grow,
and the heat
and the pressure
inside got so great
that something *new* happened,
something first rate!

15

"*What happened?*
What happened?
You've got my attention!
Please tell me,
please tell me,
of this star invention!"

"And what *is* this stuff?
Of *what* are stars made?
Is it goop, or sloop,
or sweet lemonade?"

"And would a million Earths
turn into a star,
if you strung them together
on a cosmic guitar?"

17

"Or what if you had
ten zillion ZONKS
and zipped them
together with
gaggles of GONKS?

Then, *then* would you
have built a star?
Or maybe just something
that's really bizarre?

What is it, *inside*,
that makes a star glow?
What is it?
What is it?
And how do we know?"

Back to Earth, come with me,
and I will explain.
Back to Earth, come with me,
it's really quite plain.

Let me show to you something
that's really quite neat.
Let me show to you something
that's oh, *such a treat!*

Now, when you heat up some stuff
so hot that it glows,
and look at that light
through a prism, it shows
that light is made up
of a spectrum of colors
like red and blue
and so many others.

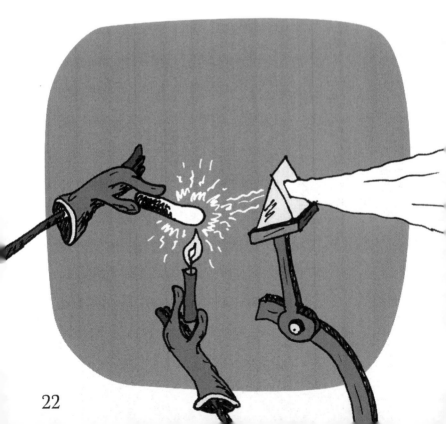

Strange lines you will see
through this prism of yours,
now heat up *more* stuff
from ten different stores!
And you'll find that each thing
has signature lines,
and you'll find that deep down
there are 92 kinds . . .

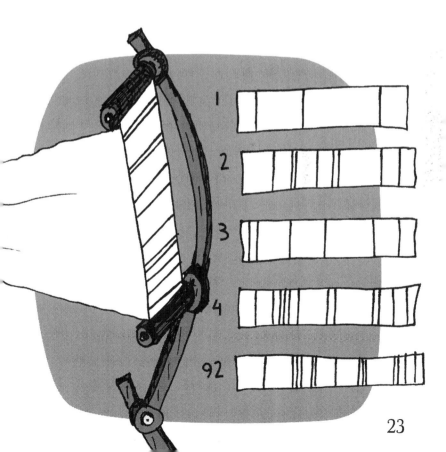

92 elements
make up all stuff –
stuff that is smooth,
or brittle, or rough,
like COPPER and ZINC
  (these make brass),
and SILICON, OXYGEN
  (these make glass).
GOLD is an element,
and HELIUM gas,
and HYDROGEN
(which is the gas
that you pass).

He
Heliu
B
C
N
O
F
Ne
OXYGEN
Al
Si
Silic
P
S
Cl
Ar
Ni
COPPER
ZINC
Ga
Ge
As
Se
Br
Kr
Ag
Cd
In
Sn
Sb
Te
I
Xe
Hg
Tl
Pb
Bi
Po
At
Rn
U
92

And *guess what*,
when you look
at the light from a star,
no matter how big,
how near, or how far,
through a prism you'll see
the very same lines,
the very same colors,
the same bright designs.
The stuff that's on stars,
so hot and so bright,
is the same kind of stuff
that's on Earth, *that's right!*

And not just on stars
but all over the place –
on planets, and comets,
and scattered through space.
The same kind of stuff
that makes up *you*
makes galaxies far, far away!
It's *true*!

But there's one more thing
that's oh, so essential
if you want to make something
with *stellar* potential . . .

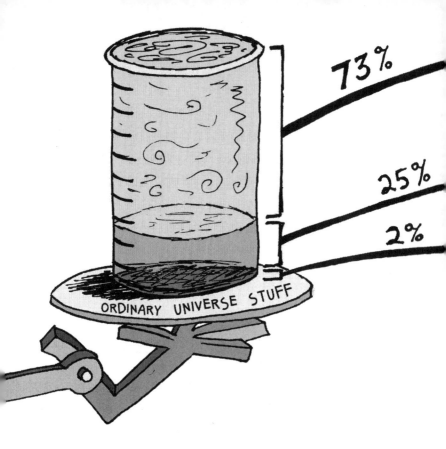

You see, it just so happens
that *most* of this stuff
is HYDROGEN gas,
there's more than enough.
73% of the stuff all around
is HYDROGEN gas,
and *that* is profound.

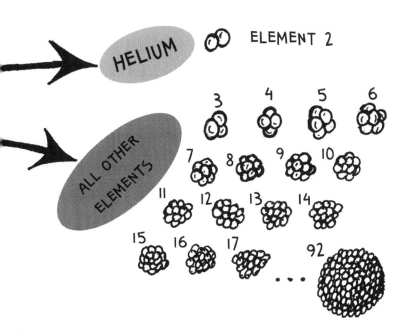

HYDROGEN, yes,
a most simple thing,
like letters in a word
or beads on a string.

HYDROGEN, yes,
it's ELEMENT ONE,
and *this* is what happens
deep down in the sun . . .

You see, in a star,
that *HYDROGEN* stuff –
it gets crushed together,
like a mountain of fluff!

And so strong is the force
that it *fuses* that mass,
it *FUSES* that mass
and it makes a *new* gas.

The simplest thing
becomes something new –
element ONE becomes
element TWO!

But most magic of all,
when this fusion sticks
a great burst of *light*
comes out of the mix.
Some of that mass,
a teeny small piece,
has turned into energy
and is released!

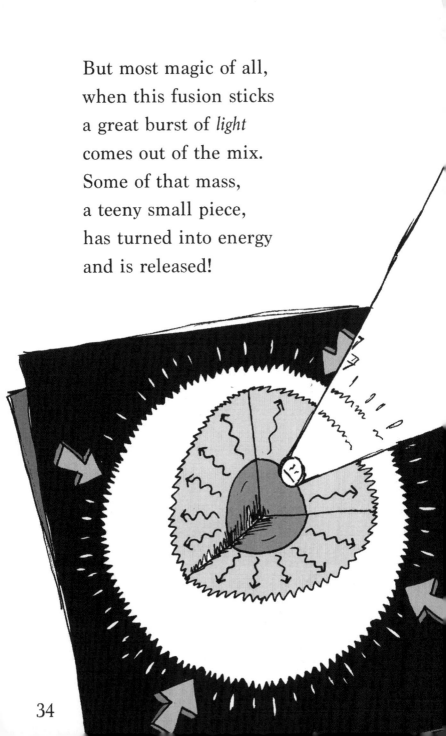

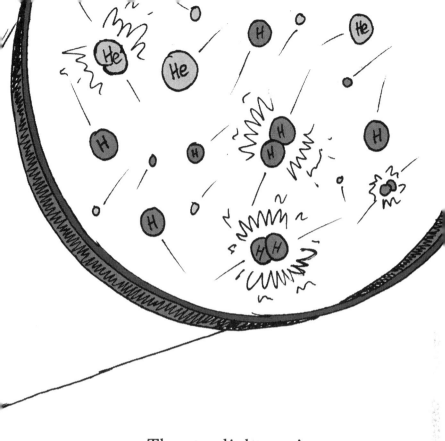

The star lights up!
It glows and glows
for ten *billion* years or so
we suppose –
if the star is about
the size of our sun.

Do you have any questions,
maybe just one?

"DR. SNOYT, you said
there are *clouds* up in space.
Where did they come from,
this SPACE-CLOUD VASE?"

GIANT
MOLECULAR
SPACE CLOUDS

DARK MATTER

GALAXIES

NEBULAE

37

Ah, yes, ah, yes. I *did* say that.
But before I explain,
we have to go back –
way back in time
to the *very* beginning,
before Earth was here
and let alone spinning.
Way back when everything,
all that you see,
was crammed into space
the size of this pea.
And *everything, all* was energy
of the highest, highest density.

Then 13.8 billion years ago,
is when it began,
this universe show.
You see, that pea grew –
inflated, we say –
BANG! it got bigger
and *fast*, by the way.

And a funny thing happened –
small *bits* popped out,
like QUARKS, and GLUONS,
and ZIBBLE-DEE-ZOUTS.

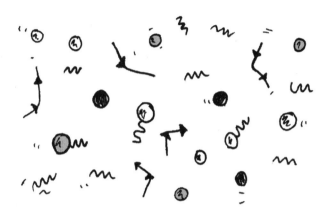

And those QUARKS grouped together,
in groups of three,
and made things called PROTONS,
now do you see?

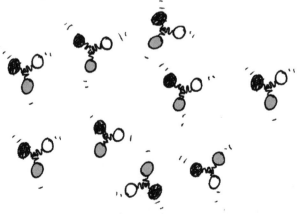

And PROTONS make elements,
like bricks make a wall.
And one proton makes HYDROGEN,
the smallest element of all.

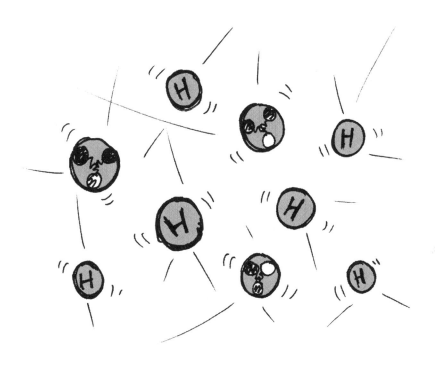

So all that hydrogen, yes, it's true,
came from that BIG BANG,
as the universe grew!

And that hydrogen gas
made the first clouds in space,
and gravity worked,
pulled them into place . . .

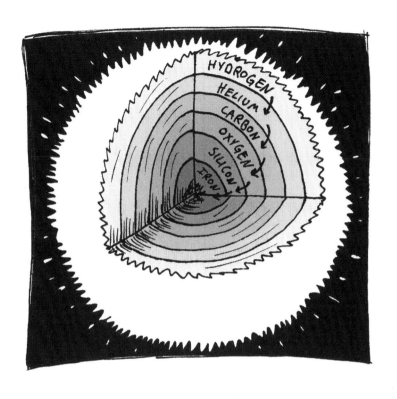

into *big* and *bright*
and *fast*-burning stars
that turned HYDROGEN stuff
into HELIUM bars,
and helium bars into CARBON stew,
and carbon stew into OXYGEN brew,
and oxygen brew into SILICON soup,
and silicon soup into IRON goop!

And all those elements
spewed right out –
scattered back into great big clouds,
no doubt!
And guess what, my friend,
formed out of *those* clouds?
More stars! It's true!
Crowds and crowds!

47

Whole *crowds* of stars
that clumped up together
in GALAXIES! CLUSTERS!
Better than ever!
And some stars lived,
and died, and exploded,
and built *more* elements –
SUPERNOVA! UNLOADED!

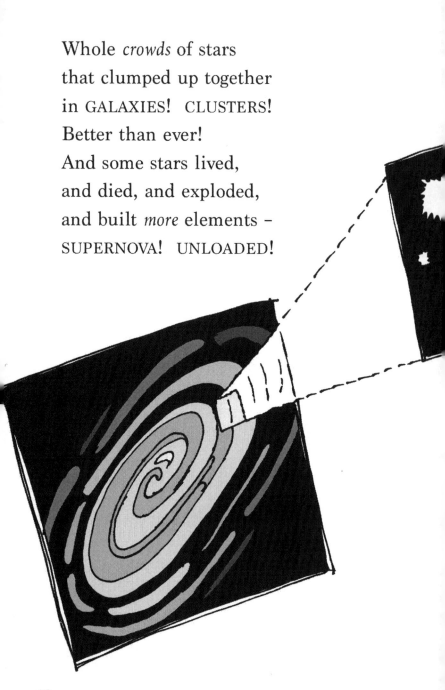

Then back into dust . . .
Space dust . . .
Space clouds . . .

And *one* of these clouds
has made me *most* proud . . .

The space-cloud that
swirled together and formed
our own Sun and its planets!
Don't be mis-informed!

Our *very* own Earth,
its dirt, and *you*,
and ZOOBLE-ZICKS,
and SNICKER-SNEWS,
the stuff we're made of,
our hands and our feet,
once lived in a star,
hey, *that's* kinda neat!

"*Kinda neat!? Kinda neat!?*
It's *amazing,* I'd say!
It's totally *great!*
A *wonderful* play!"

"But DOCTOR?
Are you just
making up words?
These are so many words
that I've never heard.

And one other thing,
you said stars exploded,
and our *Sun* is a star
that's *one* thing I've noted.
Is our Sun,
our wonderful Sun, to *blow*?
Someday in the future,
will there be a sun-snow?"

Great question, my friend,
great question, indeed!
Let me tell you some more
before we proceed.
Like ZONKS and GORKS
and SNUFFS holding SNARS,
there are many different
types of stars.

ZONK

GORK

It depends, you see,
on the size of the beast
and how much mass
showed up to the feast.

Little *red* stars
eat steady and slow
and will slowly burn out
in a *trillion* years or so.

Yellow stars,
like ours,
our very own Sun
are bigger but won't quite
explode when they're done.

Even *bigger* stars,
about ten solar masses,
eat *ten* times as much
hydrogen gasses.

    These BIG stars
    burn fast and bright,
    and hot and blue
    and even white!

Just a few million years and then,
it is these *big* stars that really KA-BLEM!

And when they blow
(like I mentioned before)
it makes all that stuff
that you get at the store.

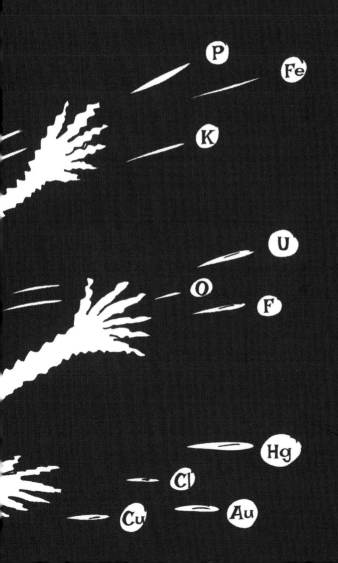

So don't worry, my friend,
our Sun won't blow-up,
at least not in the way *big* stars
go KA-BUP!
In 5 *billion* years
our Sun will morph
and live out its days
as a little WHITE DWARF.

But don't you fret, we'll be just fine,
5 billion years is *plenty* of time.

"DOCTOR, I have another question:
How much can stars *eat*
before indigestion?
Can stars get bigger
and bigger forever?
Is there an end
to this stellar endeavor?
Can you add a million *suns*
in a ball?
Or a million more?
What is the call?"

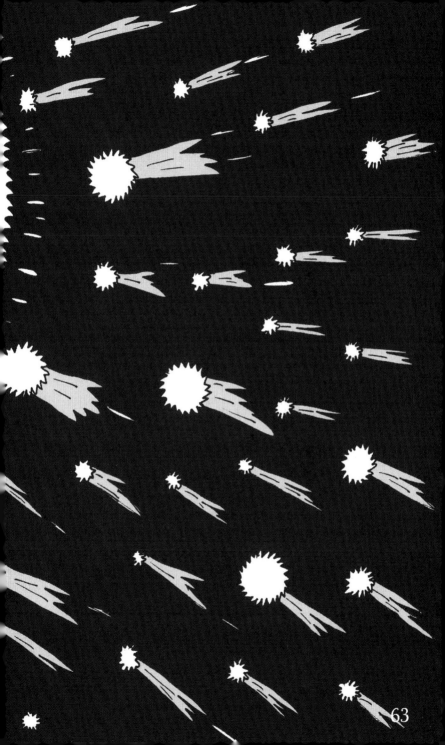

Great question, my friend,
you're very astute,
much more than ZOB
from ZOB-ZOB GALOOT,
who never asks questions
and never learns more
and lives every day
like the day lived before.

You're question is fine,
and answer I must.
There *is* a high end to stars
we've discussed!
For the bigger and bigger
and bigger the mass,
the stronger and stronger
the force, *alas!*
And that force gets so strong
a funny thing happens:
the whole thing *collapses*
and then, then it *blackens!*
That force is so strong,
that mass is so great,
that not even *light*
can escape the great weight . . .

And it forms a
SUPER MASSIVE BLACK HOLE!
A hole so black
that it *shudders* my soul!

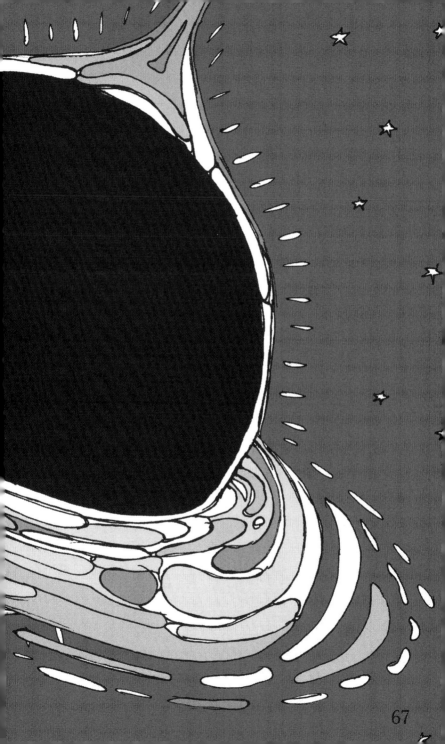

"*Wow*, DR. SNOYT!
I would like to know more –
about these *holes*
you mentioned before.
These *holes* that you say
are so very black
that nothing escapes,
nothing comes back!"

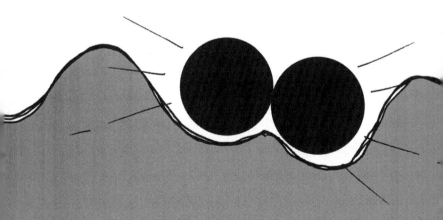

"What if these holes
crash into each other?
Does it ripple through space?
Ripple my brother?"

"And what about stuff
I've heard called NEUTRINOS?
What are they?
Is is something you win at casinos?
And what about WORM-HOLES
and MESONS and such?
Is that stuff real?
Am I asking too much?

What are QUASARS and PULSARS
and matter that's dark?
And HADRONS, and MUONS,
are those at the park?
And BOSONS and
MASSIVE COSMIC RAYS,
where are *they* found
in this sciency maze?"

My friend, *all* these things
are so very neat,
and in SCIENCE your training
is never complete.
So ask away, ask away,
each question makes more!
That's how it works
when you start to explore!

The most interesting stuff
is in the details,
like the endless layers
of a QUESTER-PILLER'S scales.
Keep asking those questions,
and go read a book!
Start down this path,
and you will be hooked!

73

And if you're in a hurry,
there's a book just for that!
ASTROPHYSICS is great,
just look at my hat!

Made in the USA
San Bernardino, CA
14 December 2018